Original title:
Cindered Accents Across the Wizard Crimp

Copyright © 2025 Swan Charm
All rights reserved.

Author: Paula Raudsepp
ISBN HARDBACK: 978-1-80559-467-3
ISBN PAPERBACK: 978-1-80559-966-1

Sorrows of the Fading Flame

In the shadowed night they quiver,
Flickers of warmth begin to slip.
Memories dance, then softly shiver,
As silence takes the candle's grip.

Once a blaze that lit the dark,
Now a glow that wanes away.
Ashes whisper, leave a mark,
Telling tales of yesterday.

A heartbeat lost within the glow,
Fragments of light begin to fade.
Longing for the fire to grow,
In a world that's too afraid.

Where laughter cracked the getting night,
Now shadows stretch their grasping hands.
The flame, a fading, fragile sight,
A memory that life demands.

Yet in the stillness, hope remains,
In every flicker, dreams ignite.
A promise carried on the strains,
To find a way back to the light.

Twilight's Farewell in Ember Winds

The sun dips low, a soft embrace,
Colors swirl in evening's breath.
Whispers carve the empty space,
In twilight's arms, we face our death.

Across the skies, the shadows play,
Grains of gold in settling dust.
They mingle softly, drift away,
In this moment, we place our trust.

With every sigh, the night unfolds,
Stories wrapped in silver threads.
Nature sleeps, the world consoled,
As beauty beckons, gently spreads.

In ember winds, the stars appear,
Kisses soft on weary eyes.
A lullaby that calms the fear,
As day departs and darkness lies.

But even as the flames will die,
There lingers warmth in every heart.
Embers whisper, never shy,
In twilight's dream, we never part.

The Magician's Sooty Serenade

Underneath the smoky veil,
A magician hums his tune.
With every note, the shadows flail,
As magic dances 'neath the moon.

Tricks unfold in whispered tones,
Colors swirl in midnight air.
Coins vanish, lost like stones,
Illusions rise, beyond compare.

With flick of wrist, a rabbit leaps,
In soot and charm, his secrets hide.
The audience, in silence, keeps,
A gasp of wonder, hearts open wide.

Yet in the dark, a sorrow sighs,
For every magic has its cost.
Behind each smile, a dream that dies,
A fleeting moment, never lost.

The serenade of smoky dreams,
Fades with the dawn, like whispered lore.
In haunted halls, the magic schemes,
As echoes linger evermore.

Glistening Ash and Arcana

In shadows deep, whispers soft,
The ember's glow, aloft and oft.
Secrets dance in twilight's haze,
While fire flickers, lost in praise.

Dust of dreams in silver air,
Echoes linger, silent prayer.
Magical realms in ashen light,
Awake the stars to spark the night.

Old tomes speak of fate's embrace,
Glistening ashes, time and space.
Through ancient wood, a whisper calls,
Arcana rises, softly falls.

Fingers trace the written lore,
Unlock a door to worlds before.
In every grain, a story burns,
A universe that forever yearns.

So heed the flames, let spirits fly,
In glistening ash, we dare to try.
With every spark, a journey starts,
Arcana's dance within our hearts.

Twilight Beneath the Sorcerer's Cloak

Beneath the veil of twilight's grace,
The sorcerer weaves in his hidden space.
Mystic patterns in the twilight glow,
Enchantment thrives where shadows flow.

Whispers of power, flickers of light,
Spells intertwine in the depth of night.
Ancient wisdom in the silken seams,
A world awash in shimmering dreams.

The stars align in secrets spun,
Guiding the lost, the chosen one.
In twilight's cloak, the tales unfold,
A magic crafted, mystique bold.

Eyes that glimmer like the dawn,
Drawn to realms where few have gone.
In the weave of fate, we find our place,
Twilight's embrace, a sacred space.

With every step, the shadows sway,
Beneath the cloak where wishes lay.
The sorcerer's heart beats ever near,
In twilight's song, we banish fear.

Phantom Flames of Forgotten Lore

Whispers weave through the silent night,
Phantom flames flicker, dancing bright.
Each spark a ghost of tales long gone,
In the shadows, spirits yawn.

Forgotten lore in embers deep,
Secrets buried, ours to keep.
Echoes linger, soft and slow,
Through the darkness, fortunes glow.

In ancient woods where shadows play,
Lost stories yearn for a new day.
With every flame, we come alive,
A spark ignites, we start to strive.

Veils of time, they shift and shimmer,
Hallways of memory faintly glimmer.
Phantom flames reveal the past,
In fleeting moments, shadows cast.

So gather 'round these flickering lights,
Embrace the lore on autumn nights.
In phantom flames, our hearts will soar,
Awakening worlds of treasured lore.

Beneath the Sooty Stars

Under skies of inky grace,
Sooty stars, a hidden face.
Dreams whisper in the smoky air,
A starlit path for souls that dare.

Night reveals its shadowed gems,
Lost horizons, whispered hems.
Each twinkle holds a story told,
In the darkness, mysteries unfold.

Beneath the watch of faded light,
The cosmos breathes, igniting night.
With every glimmer, silence speaks,
A gentle touch that nature seeks.

Footfalls soft on ashen ground,
In the quiet, truth is found.
Guided by the soot-streaked gleam,
We chase the echoes of a dream.

So let us weave our hopes anew,
Under stars, both bright and blue.
Beneath the sooty quilted sky,
We find our wings, we learn to fly.

Flickering Wishes in Midnight's Grasp

In shadows deep, the wishes dwell,
A flicker bright, a whispered spell.
Stars above, they softly gleam,
In midnight's grasp, we chase a dream.

Thoughts like fireflies dance and sway,
Through gilded night, they drift away.
Pale moonlight weaves a gentle thread,
While hope ignites, our fears are shed.

Yet midnight's breath can cool the flame,
The heart knows well this tender game.
But each desire, a fleeting spark,
Will linger on in shadows dark.

So let us take this fleeting chance,
And through the night in silence dance.
For in the dark, our wishes found,
Will light the path where dreams abound.

With every flicker, dreams arise,
In midnight's grasp, we touch the skies.
For every wish that slips away,
Leaves magic's touch in the break of day.

Songs of the Sable Spellcaster

In midnight's hush, a song takes flight,
A sable cloak in the pale moonlight.
With whispered words of ancient lore,
The spellcaster weaves magic's core.

Her voice, a breeze through willow trees,
Carries secrets on the gentle seas.
Each note is stitched in shadow's thread,
Where dreams are born and fears have fled.

The music swells, enchantments rise,
Beneath the watchful, starry skies.
A cadence of the night unfolds,
In harmony, the heart beholds.

With every song, the darkness sways,
As magic sparkles in the haze.
A sable cloak 'round wisdom's fire,
Awakens souls to hope's desire.

So listen close to the spell she sings,
In every note, the fortune brings.
For in the shadows where she roams,
The sable spellcaster finds her homes.

Forgotten Wands of Soot and Spark

In dusty corners, wands lay still,
Forgotten tales, a haunted thrill.
Crafted once with care and love,
Now cloaked in shadows from above.

Soot and spark, the essence blend,
The language lost, no tongue to lend.
Yet whispers linger in the air,
Of magic strong, of hearts laid bare.

With each long sigh, the memories fade,
Of dreams once bright, now softly laid.
But every wand holds history,
Like fading ink from ancient mystery.

To grasp a wand is to ignite,
A piece of hope in darkest night.
For every spark, a story grows,
In soot and ashes, magic flows.

So scour the dust, unearth the old,
Let forgotten wands be bought and sold.
For with each touch, the past will start,
To weave its magic in every heart.

The Embered Tapestry of Starlit Night

A tapestry where starlight weaves,
With threads of gold, the night believes.
Embers glow in a gentle embrace,
Each star a story, a luminous trace.

In twilight's grasp, the colors blend,
As day to night begins to bend.
With every flicker, fate ignites,
In the embered dance of starlit nights.

The nightingale sings to the moon's cool glow,
While whispers of magic in breezes flow.
In this canvas where dreams collide,
The heart finds peace, the soul's a guide.

From deep indigo to shimmering light,
Each thread a hope, a wish in flight.
The stars, they guide our wayward hearts,
In this tapestry, where love imparts.

So linger long in the night's embrace,
Where embered dreams find their rightful place.
For starlit skies and whispered sighs,
Unravel tales where the spirit flies.

The Enigma of Sooty Spells

In shadows dance the whispers low,
A charmed silence starts to grow.
With flickering lights, the secrets weave,
As dusk descends, the night deceives.

Cloaked in dark, the visions stir,
Mystical songs that softly blur.
Through twisted paths, the echoes trail,
In the heart of night, the magic hails.

A tapestry of whispers spun,
With every flicker, a deed begun.
The sooty ink of fate's caress,
Embroidered tales of dark distress.

To conjure dreams from whispered air,
With every glance, a hidden snare.
For those who seek, the shadows yearn,
While secrets form in pages turned.

Near glowing coals, the spirits play,
In the quiet, the lost souls sway.
With gentle hands, we grasp the thread,
A sooty script on paths we tread.

Dreams Adrift on the Fiery Breeze

Where flames entwine with drifting dreams,
A world aglow, as twilight gleams.
The fervent heat ignites the night,
With shadows dancing, hearts take flight.

Beneath the stars, the embers spark,
Guiding lost souls through the dark.
With each warm gust, we float along,
To the echo of a distant song.

Winds of fire whisper low,
Carrying tales the ancients know.
As dreams take shape in the smoky haze,
We wander through the fiery maze.

In every flicker, stories hide,
Adventures bound on the currents wide.
With steadfast hearts, we chase the flame,
In pursuit of hope, we play the game.

Embrace the night, let spirits soar,
Together, we'll seek forevermore.
For in this dance of fire and air,
We find our truth, and leave our care.

Elixirs Born from Embered Haze

In potion's glow, the world ignites,
With embered dreams in starry nights.
A swirl of colors, secrets blend,
As magic brews, the visions mend.

Through smoky trails, the aromas rise,
Invoking tales from distant skies.
In silver cauldrons, hopes ignite,
With every swirl, transforming light.

The alchemist's touch, a fiery grace,
Unveils the wonders time won't erase.
From embered hues, elixirs flow,
In every drop, the stories grow.

Crafted with care, the potion swirls,
Invoking dreams of distant worlds.
With whispered charms and timeless art,
Each sip ignites the beating heart.

As haze encircles, the spirits sway,
In this creation, we find our way.
For in each potion's glowing embrace,
We uncover our truest place.

The Sorcery of Ashen Remnants

From ashes cold, a story starts,
With whispered spells, and beating hearts.
The remnants speak in muted tones,
Of ancient magic carved in stones.

Transformed by fire, the world regrows,
In soft repose, the spirit flows.
Unraveling tales of loss and gain,
From what was burned, much will remain.

Through ashen skies, the shadows roam,
Where echoes linger, spirits comb.
In every spark, the past ignites,
A dance of echoes through the nights.

In every crumble, wisdom stays,
A legacy of embers' blaze.
With gentle hands, we gather all,
To trace the shadows, hear the call.

As seasons change, the cycle spins,
In the heart of night, the journey begins.
For in the sooty trails we seek,
The sorcery that makes us unique.

Firelit Tales in Forgotten Realms

In shadows deep where whispers dwell,
A flicker of hope weaves tales to tell.
Embers dance with stories old,
Firelit visions of worlds untold.

With every spark, a dream ignites,
Casting warmth on chilly nights.
Figures move in the glow's embrace,
Echoes of laughter fill the space.

Beneath the stars, the spirits sigh,
As glowing tales drift and fly.
The past and present intertwine,
In forgotten realms where we align.

Through time we wander, side by side,
In firelit dreams, we take our ride.
A tapestry of light and shade,
In tales of wonder, we're unafraid.

So gather 'round this flick'ring blaze,
Let stories flow in endless ways.
In every heart, a spark resides,
In firelit nights, magic abides.

The Dance of the Ashen Muse

In twilight's grip, the ashes sway,
A muse emerges to light the way.
With every step, the embers glow,
A dance of shadows, soft and slow.

Her whispers linger in the air,
Crafting dreams from thin despair.
Each graceful turn, a tale begun,
In the fiery dusk, we are one.

The ashen breeze sings through the trees,
Carrying hopes on gentle knees.
A rhythm found in flame and night,
In whispered secrets, hearts take flight.

Around her, sparks of brilliance glide,
As memories waltz, weaving wide.
In the stillness, we feel the call,
The dance of the muse enchanting all.

So join the swirl, let spirits rise,
With every heartbeat, love defies.
In ashen light, let us embrace,
The dance of life, an endless grace.

Gossamer Threads of Enchanted Dust

In twilight's glow, a shimmer grows,
Gossamer threads where magic flows.
Whispers of faeries tease the night,
With each soft touch, our hearts take flight.

In every glimmer, stories weave,
A tapestry of dreams to believe.
Through the dust, enchantments swirl,
In fleeting visions, mysteries unfurl.

The starlit sky unveils its lore,
As echoes dance on a distant shore.
Each thread a path, a choice to make,
In woven tales, our souls awake.

With gentle hands, we trace the stars,
Embracing hope with open arms.
In every breath, we find a way,
To join the dance of night and day.

So gather close, let time unfold,
In gossamer dreams, we're brave and bold.
For in this dust, we find our trust,
In enchanted realms where spirits gust.

Traces of Thistle and Flame

In fields of thistle, shadows roam,
Echoes of fire lead us home.
Wars of whispers, hearts aflame,
In the thorns, we stake our claim.

The night is alive with longing sighs,
As flick'ring embers light the skies.
Every thorn holds a tale of old,
Of battles fought and daring bold.

Through flickering light, our paths entwine,
In every struggle, a fate divine.
With thistle strength and fire's glow,
We stand united, hearts aglow.

So in this realm where dreams collide,
Find traces of the flame inside.
With courage born from ancient strife,
We'll carve our mark upon this life.

In thistle's grasp, let passion burn,
In every lesson, hearts will learn.
Through all the scars, we'll rise again,
In traces of thistle and flame.

Cinders in the Veil of Night

In the quiet glow of twilight's breath,
Cinders dance, whispering tales of death.
Stars above shimmer, secrets they hold,
Veils of darkness, stories unfold.

Embers flicker, like ghosts in the air,
Each spark a memory, lost to despair.
Night's embrace wraps the world in its shroud,
Echoing silence, muffled and loud.

Softly they fade, like dreams long gone,
A flick of the wrist, a final yawn.
Yet in the ashes, a promise lies,
In quiet corners where hope never dies.

Threads of Ashen Whimsy

In a tapestry woven with whispers and sighs,
Threads of ash drift, like dreams in the skies.
Whimsy they carry, a jest of the past,
Echoes of laughter, shadows that cast.

Flickering flames tease the fabric of night,
Laughter ignites in the flicker of light.
Grains of time slip through nimble fingers,
In the heart of the fire, sweet joy lingers.

Woven together, in patterns of grace,
Ashen threads dance in a mystical space.
Unravel the stories behind each design,
For in every strand lies the spark of divine.

Light and Shadow in the Elderwood

Beneath the canopy where secrets reside,
Light filters softly, shadows collide.
Whispers of ancients echo through leaves,
In the heart of the woods, the magic weaves.

Every glimmer tells a story untold,
In the arms of the trees, both timid and bold.
Branches entwined, like fate's gentle touch,
Breathe in the starlight; it beckons so much.

Twilight's dance plays through the forest's embrace,
Where light and shadow find sacred space.
In silence we wander, in wonder we rest,
For the elderwood holds nature's best.

Whirling Scents of the Pyromancer's Grove

In the grove where the flames twist and twine,
Scents of the burning herbs intertwine.
A dance of the wild, a ritual's art,
Fires ignite, and the magic imparts.

Each flicker reveals a deep, hidden lore,
Whispers of pyromancers who came before.
Spices and smoke fill the air with delight,
As shadows and flames play their dance of night.

Chants resonate, carried on winds,
In the heart of the grove, where all life begins.
Whirling around, the fires embrace,
Creating a haven, a sacred space.

Embers Whispering in Arcane Shadows

In the night where secrets dwell,
Embers dance and softly swell.
Whispers curl in shadows deep,
Arcane tales the darkness keep.

A flicker speaks of ancient lore,
Echoes of those gone before.
In the silence, magic stirs,
Unlocking dreams with silent purrs.

Crimson sparks like fireflies,
Illuminate the midnight skies.
Each glow a promise, sweet and rare,
In the world of whispered air.

Mystic voices call from night,
Guiding souls toward the light.
With every crackle, every sigh,
The embers beckon, time to fly.

So dance with shadows, heed the flame,
Embrace the quiet, call the names.
For in this realm of twilight mist,
The magic waits, it can't be missed.

Enchanted Whispers of Ashen Tongues

In the twilight's soft embrace,
Ashen tongues leave not a trace.
Whispers rise like smoke in air,
Enchanting dreams, a secret care.

Every flicker tells a tale,
Of forgotten quests and trails.
Voices linger, faint yet clear,
In the echoes, magic near.

The shadows hum a lullaby,
As stars awake in velvet sky.
With every breath of fading light,
The whispers weave through endless night.

From the ashes, hope will bloom,
Casting away the weight of gloom.
In the heart of silence spun,
Enchantment whispers, softly done.

So listen close, let dreams ascend,
On ashen tongues, the stories bend.
For in the whispers, find the key,
To realms of magic, wild and free.

The Spellbound Soot of Forgotten Realms

In the corners of lost dreams,
Spellbound soot, where nothing seems.
Tall tales linger, floating slow,
In realms where only shadows go.

The dust of ages softly sighs,
Holding secrets, ancient ties.
With each breath, the past ignites,
Creating worlds of starry nights.

Forgotten realms, both near and far,
Glimmers hide like hidden stars.
Through the gloom, a pathway glows,
Where only the brave dare to go.

Every whisper speaks of change,
In this realm, both wild and strange.
To wander forth is to embrace,
The magic time cannot erase.

So take the soot, allow it to weave,
A tapestry of all we believe.
In forgotten realms, truths unfold,
In the silence, wonders told.

Flickering Flames on Eldritch Paths

On the edge of night's decree,
Flickering flames call out to me.
Eldritch paths of whispers glow,
Guiding steps where few dare go.

A gentle flicker sways like dreams,
Veiled in magic's muted schemes.
Each flame a beacon, fierce yet kind,
Leading forth to what we find.

Through the darkness, courage grows,
As the fire's warmth gently flows.
With every heartbeat, shadows play,
In enchantment's soft ballet.

Mystical flames spark the night,
Breathing life to dormant light.
Every flicker, every spark,
Illuminates the hidden dark.

So take this journey, brave and bold,
Through the paths where tales are told.
Flickering flames guide the way,
To realms where dreams will never fray.

Specters of Charred Wishes

In the ashes, dreams do dwell,
Whispers of hopes that once fell.
Flickered flames, a ghostly dance,
Beneath the night's somber trance.

Fallen embers, tales untold,
Visions of futures turned cold.
Wishes drift on winds of time,
Echoes of laughter in a chime.

Figures rise from the burnt remains,
Haunting shadows, lingering chains.
Promises made now turn to dust,
In the fire, we placed our trust.

The night carries a somber tune,
Melodies lost beneath the moon.
Specters roam in search of light,
Clutching dreams that fade from sight.

Yet in darkness, seeds can grow,
From scattered ash, new hope can show.
With each spark, we'll light the way,
To forge our wishes anew each day.

The Sorcerer's Charcoal Muse

In shadows deep, the sorcerer stirs,
With charcoal wand, the magic blurs.
A world of ink, his canvas spreads,
Where fantasy walks where logic treads.

He sketches dreams in midnight hue,
With breath of fire, visions anew.
Each stroke ignites the heart's desire,
Enchanting souls with whispered fire.

Figures dance in the flickering light,
Ghostly forms in the still of night.
Wonders crafted from darkened air,
With every spell, he casts a snare.

In charcoal night, the stories weave,
Of loves lost and what we believe.
A twist of fate, a hand so bold,
Creates a tale that must be told.

Through ash and smoke, the spirits rise,
In the sorcerer's realm, the world lies.
With every charred dream, he renews,
His heart ablaze, a muse he brews.

So let the fire light our way,
In charcoal dreams, we shall stay.
For every wish that sparks a flame,
We find our passion, we find our name.

Beneath the Blackened Moon

Beneath the moon, so black and bare,
Whispers linger in the chilling air.
Night swallows secrets, silent and deep,
In shadows where the lost ones weep.

Silhouettes crawl in the muted glow,
From realms of dreams where sorrows flow.
Echoes ripple through the still night,
Where hopes linger and take flight.

The stars are ghosts in a smoky mist,
Holding tales of the dreams we've missed.
Each flicker a wish, faded yet bright,
A promise reborn with the dawn's light.

In haunted corners where silence reigns,
Reverberations of joy and pain.
With every breath, the darkness sighs,
Beneath the moon, a world defies.

Yet from the depths of despair and gloom,
Life finds a way to once more bloom.
For every shadow that casts a spell,
Holds stories waiting, heartbeats to tell.

The Weaving of Fiery Shadows

In a realm where shadows dance free,
Fiery weavers spin destiny.
Threads of light entwined with night,
Crafting tales that shine so bright.

Each flicker a story yet to unfold,
Whispers of courage, dreams bold.
Through the haze, a path appears,
In the tapestry of hopes and fears.

Shadows whisper in the twilight air,
Of journeys taken, dreams laid bare.
With every twist, the patterns grow,
In the dark, the embers glow.

Weaving hopes with threads of fate,
Creating futures, we celebrate.
For in each shadow, there's a spark,
Guiding us through the endless dark.

So let the weavers pitch their loom,
In the fire's dance, we find our room.
For every shadow, a story spun,
In fiery weavings, we'll become one.

In the silence, the echoes call,
To unite the dreams of us all.
In the weaving of fiery shadows,
Together we rise, we will not fall.

The Charred Medallion's Whisper

In the depths of night, it glows,
A secret kept where darkness flows.
Whispers dance on ember's breath,
Tales of love, betrayal, death.

Fingers trace its tarnished face,
Hearing echoes of a lost embrace.
Threads of fate entwined in gold,
Promises whispered, stories told.

Shadows drape the ancient stone,
Guarding tales of hearts now lone.
A flicker speaks of times gone by,
Silent witnesses to the sky.

The fire wanes, the embers fade,
Memories in the twilight laid.
Yet the medallion's glow remains,
Binding souls through joy and pains.

Restless dreams beneath the stars,
Chasing echoes, healing scars.
In the charred medallion's sigh,
Lies the truth that can't deny.

The Sorceress's Flickering Heart

In shadows deep, her power spins,
A twilight dance where magic begins.
Flickering sparks in her gaze,
A world ignited in secret ways.

Her heart a beacon, fragile light,
Guiding lost souls through the night.
A flick of wrist, a whispered chant,
Grasping hope, as dreams recant.

The storm it brews, with tempest's grace,
She conjures storms to hide her face.
Yet in her core, warmth gently glows,
A flickering heart that only she knows.

With every spell, a piece laid bare,
A longing heart beneath the glare.
Love entwined with shadows spun,
A battle fought, yet never won.

In twilight's hush, her visions flare,
A sorceress lost in her own despair.
Yet in the dark, her spirit finds
A flickering heart that love unwinds.

Light woven in Ashen Shadows

In the ruins where embers lie,
New patterns form beneath the sky.
Light weaves through ashen frames,
Crafting whispers of forgotten names.

As shadows stretch, the past ignites,
Reclaiming dreams from endless nights.
Ghostly hands in the twilight play,
Painting colors where night held sway.

Each flickering glow, a tale retold,
Of love once bright, of hearts still bold.
In the quiet, truth takes flight,
Light woven in the depth of night.

The ashes settle, yet hope remains,
In every shadow, a pulse contains.
Threads of drama in the woven dark,
Guiding lost souls with a gentle spark.

Though time may fade and silence call,
The woven light will never fall.
Ashen shadows breathe life anew,
In every heart, a story true.

The Sinister Glow of Forgotten Lore

In the heart of the wood, a whisper clings,
Secrets hidden beneath dark wings.
A sinister glow beckons the brave,
Tales waiting in the shadows to save.

Forgotten lore in every breeze,
Stirring murmurs among the trees.
Echoes of wisdom long since lost,
Riddles wound tight—at what cost?

The night unfolds with a chilling sigh,
As ancient truths begin to fly.
Each flicker of light tells a part,
Of love and hate entwined in heart.

In the ruins where silence reigns,
An urge to know, despite the pains.
For the glow warns, yet still invites,
To dance with shadows in the nights.

Through twisted paths, the seeker goes,
Chasing shadows, where the sinister glows.
In forgotten lore lies a chance to see,
The balance of dark and light, to be free.

Alchemy of Ash and Stardust

In shadows deep, where secrets bloom,
Whispers rise from the silent gloom.
Ashes dance on the breath of night,
Crafting stars with their fading light.

Time entwines in a delicate weave,
Regrets like smoke, we toil and heave.
Yet in the blend of despair and grace,
Hope ignites in this sacred space.

From ember's trace, the magic grows,
Transforming hearts, where passion flows.
With every breath, a tale reborn,
In the stillness, our spirits worn.

We gather dreams from ashes lost,
A carousel where shadows tossed.
Through the veil of twilight's song,
We find the place where we belong.

In alchemy's heart, we dare to play,
With dust of stars, we light the way.
Embracing all, the night unfolds,
In every tale, the universe holds.

Flames of the Lost Incantation

In twilight's grasp, the whispers call,
Forgotten spells in shadows fall.
With flickering light, the secrets tease,
As flames take flight on a chilling breeze.

Fingers trace along the flame,
Seeking echoes, carving names.
Incantations lost, yet softly heard,
Within the fire, each word disturbed.

Yearning hearts grasp for the past,
In flickering glow, the shadows cast.
Memories weave through the smoky allure,
Binding the lost to the uncertain pure.

Embers whisper tales of despair,
Of love once held, now lost in air.
With every rise, a grief unseen,
Inside the blaze where we once dreamed.

Yet still the fire invites the night,
A dance of spirits, a flickering light.
Through loss, we find our strength anew,
In the flames, our souls break through.

The Enchanted Ember's Lament

In moments steeped in sorrow's grace,
An ember glows, a wistful trace.
Once vibrant flames, now softly sigh,
A lament echoing through the sky.

Hushed whispers speak of tales once told,
Of love and loss in the crisp, cold.
Each flicker holds a fleeting spark,
A memory's glow in the endless dark.

With flickering tongues, they dance and weep,
For promises made, now buried deep.
Yet in their light, we still believe,
In magic's grace we can receive.

In shadows play the ghosts of past,
Where every ember's warmth will last.
A heartbeat thrums in the twilight's hush,
As dreams arise in the midnight rush.

The enchanted ember, though bittersweet,
Holds the promise of love complete.
With every flicker, our hearts unite,
In the glow, we find our light.

Echoes from the Pyre of Dreams

Upon the pyre where dreams once soared,
Whispers linger, their voices roared.
In clouds of smoke, past wishes dwell,
Each crackle tells a silent spell.

The ember's glow reveals the night,
A canvas painted in firelight.
Fading visions drift through the air,
While time entwines each passionate prayer.

Through ashes grey, a story spins,
Of hope ignited where darkness begins.
With every spark, a memory wakes,
In the heart of the flame, the future aches.

Echoes dance on the edges of fate,
Carving paths where dreams await.
Through warm embrace, we seek the dawn,
In the ashes of what once was gone.

So gather round the glimmering fire,
To lift our hopes, to chase desire.
For every flicker tells a tale,
In the pyre's glow, our hearts prevail.

Embers of Enchantment

In twilight's glow, the fire sighs,
Soft whispers dance beneath the skies.
Each spark, a tale of dreams once bright,
An echo of the fading light.

Memories flicker, shadows play,
Captured in the gold of day.
With every crackle, a soft plea,
For lost moments to be set free.

Through glowing ash, the magic twirls,
As night unfurls her velvet curls.
A tapestry of wishes spun,
In the warmth where dreams begun.

The flames remind us of our past,
In every ember, love amassed.
We gather close, our faces near,
As warmth sings softly in the ear.

The charmed allure, it draws us close,
Where dreams and fire together dose.
In the heart of night, we ignite,
The embers of enchantment's light.

Whispers of Charred Spells

In shadows deep, where echoes dwell,
The air is thick with charred spells.
A haunting lullaby takes flight,
In the stillness of the night.

Words of smoke swirl in the air,
Carried forth in whispered prayer.
Each flickering tongue, a secret shared,
In the ancient woods, souls bared.

The heat will guide our steps anew,
While shadows twist in every hue.
With every breath, the magic swells,
In the night where the heart compels.

Around us twinkle stars so rare,
The universe listens with care.
Like fireflies in a darkened sky,
Charred spells linger, floating by.

When dawn arrives, the spells will fade,
Yet in our hearts, they're gently laid.
In the embers' glow, we'll hold tight,
To whispers of enchanted night.

Shadows in the Sorcerer's Forge

Deep in the dark where shadows creep,
The sorcerer's forge conceals secrets deep.
With hammers striking, and fires roar,
Mystic creations, forever more.

Steel bends slowly in the heated dance,
As whispers of magic take their chance.
Each flicker of flame, each twist of fate,
Gives rise to the dreams we contemplate.

Within the shadows, spirits dwell,
Crafting enchantments, weaving a spell.
Old tales echo through the gloom,
In the sorcerer's forge, shadows bloom.

A cauldron brews with essence pure,
Mysterious potions, allure obscure.
As night descends, our hearts explore,
The shadows in the sorcerer's lore.

With every strike of hammer's song,
The magic whispers, where we belong.
In the furnace's glow, secrets ignite,
Shadows of wonder fill the night.

The Ashen Melody

In the stillness, a melody plays,
Crafted in twilight's amber haze.
Notes soft as ash on the breeze,
Whispering tales with effortless ease.

The burn of fire, a gentle tune,
Under the watchful, glowing moon.
Each chord a spark of memory bright,
In the dance of shadows, hearts take flight.

Love lingers long in the smoky air,
A symphony of losses laid bare.
From flickered flames, the music swells,
In the heart of night, the ashen bells.

Kindled warmth, it draws us nigh,
Each ashen note a whispered sigh.
Together we sway, in soft embrace,
Caught in the warmth of a timeless grace.

As dawn approaches with gentle light,
The melody fades, slipping from sight.
Yet in our dreams, it will remain,
The ashen melody's sweet refrain.

The Whispering Ember's Dance

In the hearth's warm glow, shadows sway,
Softly flickering, they lead the way.
A dance of whispers in the night,
Embers twirl, a gentle light.

The air is thick with tales untold,
Of dreams and hopes, of daring bold.
Around the flames, secrets don't lie,
They ignite the heart, and the soul will fly.

Each crackle sings of worlds unknown,
In the warmth, we find what we've grown.
Fleeting moments embraced by fire,
A timeless bond, a shared desire.

As embers fade into the dark,
Memories linger, each subtle spark.
Caught in the dance of heat and glow,
We find our light in the ebb and flow.

Magic Born of Smoke

Puffs of grey weave through the air,
Mystic forms that twist with flair.
A spell of vision, a glimpse of fate,
Within the smoke, we contemplate.

Each wisp a whisper, a tale reborn,
From silent dreams, new worlds are sworn.
Magic flows where shadows gleam,
In every plume, a living dream.

Gathered around the curling mist,
We seek the wonders we can't resist.
As visions dance in hazy grace,
We lose ourselves in time and space.

So let the smoke rise, let it soar,
Open the heart, unlock the door.
With every breath, we discover more,
A magic woven forevermore.

Fragments of a Singing Flame

Sparks ignite, a symphony bright,
Each flicker sings, a pure delight.
In the hearth, a heart beats strong,
   Notes of fire weave a song.

The flames leap high, a dance of cheer,
Whispers of warmth, they draw us near.
In every crackle, a story's told,
Of passion burning, fierce and bold.

As shadows play on the cabin's wall,
The rhythm swells, a beckoning call.
Fragments of laughter in the air,
Moments cherished, beyond compare.

The night may fade, the fire may die,
   Yet in our hearts, the echoes lie.
For each flame that sang, though it may cease,
   Leaves behind a shared peace.

The Scribe of Embered Tomes

In the twilight, by firelight's grace,
A scribe records in this sacred space.
With quill poised above the page,
Stories born from the embered stage.

Words unfurl like the smoke's own flight,
Capturing whispers of long-lost night.
Each letter glows, a radiant mark,
Illuminating the once hidden dark.

The pages turn with a soft, warm sigh,
Chronicles born as the flames reach high.
A tapestry woven of hope and despair,
In the ink, they dance, alive in the air.

Each tome a keeper of tales so grand,
Of heroes, lovers, a timeless band.
As the scribe writes under starlit dome,
Embers gleam, a guiding home.

Whispers of the Pyre's Art

In shadows deep, the fire breathes,
A dance of flames, a voice that weaves.
Whispers rise with sparks that fly,
Stories old, as night drifts by.

Embers glow with secrets shared,
Of dreams and hopes both bold and scared.
Cinders hum a haunting tune,
Beneath the watchful, silver moon.

Flickers play upon the ground,
Where lost souls seek, and truth is found.
Each crackle sings of life's embrace,
In glowing warmth, we find our place.

The pyre's heart beats wild and free,
A canvas 'neath the stars at sea.
Crafted in the flames' bright thrall,
Existence folds within their call.

So gather close and hear the fire,
In every flame lies pure desire.
With open heart and mind take part,
In the whispers of the pyre's art.

Charcoal Myths Beneath the Veil

In the ash, the stories dwell,
Charcoal myths, where echoes tell.
Veiled in shadows, old and wise,
Truths emerge as darkness flies.

Each stroke of black draws forth the past,
In fleeting moments, shadows cast.
Fragments linger, soft yet strong,
A hush that hums the ancient song.

Mystic tales of light and dark,
Dance in embers, leaving mark.
A tapestry of smoke entwined,
In this realm, our fates aligned.

Through the charcoal, visions spark,
A whispered truth that leaves its mark.
In fleeting breaths, the night reveals,
The myths beneath, the heart that heals.

So linger close, breathe in the night,
Charcoal dreams take wing in flight.
In every myth, a story's pulse,
Beneath the veil, our spirits lulse.

Incantations Entwined in Cinders

Softly spoken, shadows sway,
Incantations guide the way.
Twisted words in flickered flame,
Feel the power, call a name.

Cinders dance with ancient grace,
In their warmth, we find our place.
Eldritch whispers fill the air,
Secrets shared, both rich and rare.

With every spark, the night ignites,
Mysteries within our sights.
In the glow, our fears are shed,
Incantations softly said.

Unraveled truths in glowing light,
Cindered dreams take joyous flight.
With courage found in embers bright,
We trace the magic of the night.

So gather 'round and listen close,
Let the flames spell out a prose.
Incantations, deep and tender,
In cinders' grasp, our hearts surrender.

A Tapestry of Heat and Mystery

Threads of fire weave through the dark,
A tapestry, igniting spark.
Heat embraces each twisted tale,
In every knot, a hidden trail.

Mystery cloaked in flickering light,
Dance of shadows, whispering night.
Patterns form in fiery dance,
Drawing hearts to take a chance.

In woven strands, our fates entwine,
Each heartbeat echoes, pure design.
With every glow, our spirits rise,
In the warmth, we seek the skies.

So let the fire tell its lore,
In each ember, we yearn for more.
A tapestry of heat and grace,
In every flame, we find our place.

Join the dance and feel the heat,
Within the flames, our dreams repeat.
A mystery held in gentle sway,
A tapestry that will not fray.

Inked in Flames

In the dark, shadows dance,
Whispers of the fire's chance.
Words like embers on the page,
Fueling thoughts in a burning cage.

A brush kissed by the light,
Crafts tales in the dead of night.
Ink flowing like molten gold,
Secrets of the brave and bold.

Each stroke a flicker of fate,
Stories weaved beneath the weight.
Pages turning with a sigh,
Echoes of dreams that soar and fly.

Flames flicker, shadows tease,
Carving out the poet's pleas.
With every spark, a heart ignites,
Inked in flames, the soul invites.

Bound by passion, lost in time,
Verses reach their sacred prime.
A journey wrought from heart's desire,
In the ink, a burning fire.

The Enchanted Grimoire of Smoke's Embrace

In the twilight, whispers call,
Ancient secrets, hidden thrall.
Pages filled with arcane lore,
A mystic scent from the smoke's core.

Woven spells in shadows deep,
Guarding dreams that softly sleep.
With a flick, the magic flows,
In the grimoire, pure power glows.

Veils of mist, a gentle veil,
Rising softly, telling tales.
Each word conjures the unknown,
Paths of fate and seeds are sown.

In every curl, a story brews,
Crafted tales, the heart renews.
Unseen forces, spirits rise,
With the smoke, the truth defies.

Turn the page, let the sparks fly,
In the embrace of mystic sky.
Grimoire's heart, where shadows twine,
In the smoke, the stars align.

A Flickering Heart Amidst the Flames

A heart beats in the embers' glow,
Flickering softly, just like so.
Amidst the heat, a spirit yearns,
In the fire, a lesson burns.

With every crackle, courage grows,
The flame reveals what silence knows.
A dance of shadows in the night,
Fueling hope, igniting light.

In the blaze of passion's grace,
Flickers of life, a warm embrace.
The heart, aflame with dreams so bold,
Whispers of stories yet untold.

Rising smoke, a gentle sigh,
Carving paths as moments fly.
In the flicker, souls collide,
Amidst the flames, we cannot hide.

Breathe the warmth, let fears decay,
In the fire, we find our way.
Flickering heart, forever tame,
In the blaze, we share a name.

Chronicles of the Sooty Sage

In the shadows, wisdom lies,
The sooty sage reads the skies.
Tales of ages etched in grime,
Echoes soft as whispered chime.

With a quill made of ash and smoke,
Every word, a timeless cloak.
Chronicles of life unfold,
In the soot, the truth is told.

Through the haze, memories burn,
Guiding us at every turn.
Lessons learned, and visions clear,
In the sage's heart, we draw near.

Elders speak in fiery tones,
Knowledge rests in ancient bones.
Each chapter holds a spark divine,
In the soot, the stars align.

From shadows deep, the light shall rise,
The sooty sage, both wise and wise.
Through chronicles crafted with care,
In this journey, wisdom's dare.

Residue of Magic in Ashen Hues

In twilight's grasp, whispers fade,
Echoes of spells, solemnly laid.
Soft shadows flicker, secrets untold,
In ashen hues, the magic grows bold.

Leaves rustle gently, aglow with dreams,
Crimson and gold in moonlight's beams.
A flicker of hope from the embers' bright,
Residue glimmers on the edge of night.

Distant chants rise from the nightingale,
Carried by winds through a whispering veil.
Each spark a story, each ember a sigh,
Awakening magic that will never die.

Cloaked figures dance in the soft, hazy light,
Weaving connections unseen to the sight.
In ash-laden winds, the old legends swirl,
While the residue of magic begins to unfurl.

And when the dawn breaks, fading away,
The essence of night will still softly stay.
In shadows it lingers, a delicate trace,
The residue of magic, a timeless embrace.

Haze of Ancient Charms in Gloom

In the depth of night where the shadows creep,
Ancient charms lie in secrets we keep.
Haze blankets the world in a soft, warm glow,
Unraveling tales of the long-ago.

Through twisted branches and overgrown trails,
The spirit of magic in silence prevails.
Gloom whispers softly, a voice thin and sweet,
Inviting the brave to stumble and meet.

Embers of twilight meld into dreams,
Where silence sings, and the moonlight schemes.
Every rustle of leaves tells a tale of the past,
In the haze of the night, enchantment holds fast.

Faint echoes linger like songs on the breeze,
Wrapping the hearts of the wandering trees.
In the mystic embrace where old spirits croon,
The haze of ancient charms hums a soft tune.

As dawn draws near, the dreams start to fade,
Yet whispers of magic remain unafraid.
In every gust, in each fleeting room,
Lives the soft echo of that ancient gloom.

Glimmering Dust within Embered Spellcraft

Flickering lights in the stillness of night,
Glimmering dust dances, a wondrous sight.
Each particle whispers of stories untold,
Within embered spellcraft, the magic grows bold.

Traces of starlight caught in the air,
Lightly they twirl, with nary a care.
Crafted from dreams and the wishes we cast,
Their shimmer speaks volumes of times that have passed.

A cauldron brews with whispers of lore,
Every drop carries ancient tales from before.
Glimmering dust, a key to the past,
Unlocking the secrets of shadows so vast.

In the midst of the night, when the world is asleep,
These particles weave through the silence so deep.
Each glint a reminder of magic anew,
Ebbing through twilight, a delicate hue.

As dawn's fingers stretch with a gentle caress,
The glimmering dust seems to softly confess.
Though daylight arrives and the spells seem to part,
Ember's warm magic still lingers at heart.

Twilight's Dance of Smoldering Wonders

In the fading light, where the shadows lie,
Twilight beckons under an amber sky.
Smoldering wonders weave through the air,
A dance of the dusk, enchantingly rare.

Figures emerge from the depths of the night,
Cloaked in the whispers of flickering light.
Each movement a story, each glance a spell,
Coloring the dark with their magical swell.

Embers rise gently, igniting the dreams,
As time starts to wane and reality seems.
The air thick with magic, both tender and fierce,
While twilight's charms linger, ready to pierce.

The laughter of shadows echoes and spins,
While dusk brushes lightly against golden skins.
In the realm of the spellbound, moments align,
As smoldering wonders flicker and shine.

Then comes the night in a gentle embrace,
Wrapping the world in a timeless grace.
And though dawn will creep in with its bright, bold hue,
Twilight's dance will forever ring true.

Echoes of the Mystic Forge

In shadows deep, the hammers strike,
Creating shapes with sacred light.
Whispers linger in the bronze,
As ancient spirits hum their songs.

Through the flames, the visions dance,
Crafted steel in a trance.
Tales of old, in sparks arise,
Underneath the starry skies.

The anvil's song, a vibrant call,
Echoes through the hallowed hall.
Melding worlds of time and space,
In the forge's warm embrace.

With every clang, new magic forms,
In the heat of raging storms.
Artisans of fate do weave,
With each breath, their spirits cleave.

Awake the dreams from metal wrought,
In every piece, a battle fought.
From the depths, creation roars,
In the echoes of mystic forges.

Flickers in the Arcane Night

A lantern glows with a gentle flare,
Casting shadows, secrets laid bare.
In the night, the whispers flow,
Where ancient magic starts to grow.

Stars above in patterns weave,
Stories told to those who believe.
With each flicker, a tale unfolds,
Of sorcery, powers, and molds.

Beneath the moon's soft silvery sheen,
Wizards gather, their faces keen.
Chanting songs of ages past,
Hoping for the spells to last.

Cauldrons bubble, potions brew,
Harnessing dreams, both false and true.
In the arcane night, they dwell,
Finding peace in the magic's spell.

Flickers of light that dance and sway,
Guide the wanderers on their way.
For in each shadow, a secret lies,
In the arcane night, where magic flies.

Charcoal Dreams of the Mages

In the depths of twilight's gloom,
Charcoal whispers, dreams consume.
From the pages, visions rise,
Mages weaving, ancient ties.

With strokes of black on parchment white,
They sketch the worlds, a wondrous sight.
Figures dance with vibrant grace,
Traveling through both time and space.

Warding spells in every line,
Crafted deep on aged spine.
As ink flows like a river wide,
Minds expand, where wonders bide.

Fates entwined in dusky shades,
The mages' dreams, where hope cascades.
In charcoal's grip, they find their spark,
Illuminating the endless dark.

Dreams of power, of lost and found,
In charcoal whispers, magic's bound.
The mages' heart, forever true,
In every dream, the old and new.

The Firefly's Spell

In silence of the wooded glade,
The fireflies begin their parade.
Flickering lights in gentle flight,
Casting spells on the summer night.

A dance of glow in every hue,
Weaving tales of love anew.
Soft as whispers, bright as dreams,
They enchant the world with silver beams.

Gentle breezes carry their tune,
Starlit blessings from the moon.
In their glow, the darkness fades,
Kindling warmth in forest shades.

With daring twirls and vibrant turns,
The magic in their light confirms.
Each flicker holds a story shared,
A moment caught, a heart laid bare.

The firefly's spell, a fleeting glance,
In twilight's glow, we find romance.
For in their dance, we see the light,
A spark of joy in the soft night.

Charred Echoes of Enchantment

In shadows deep where whispers roam,
   The embers dance, a silent tome.
A flicker holds a dream once bright,
   Now lost within the fading light.

   Twilight's breath, a sacred sigh,
Remembers moments long gone by.
   With every crackle, tales retold,
   Of magic woven, bright and bold.

Charred echoes haunt the twilight air,
   As secrets linger, none compare.
In haunted woods, a phantom's grace,
   In every shadow, find their trace.

   Enchantment lingers in the night,
   A dance of flame, an eerie sight.
   The forest hums a gentle tune,
Beneath the watchful, silver moon.

   From ashes rise, a spirit's flight,
   To weave the tales of ancient rite.
With every breath, the magic swells,
In charred remains, our heart compels.

The Mystique of Smoldering Sorcery

In twilight's grip, the shadows breathe,
Where magic weaves and dreams bequeath.
A flame ignites the ancient night,
With whispers cloaked in ghostly light.

Violet smoke curls through the trees,
Bringing life to forgotten pleas.
Heed the call of the arcane art,
As fiery embers play their part.

Sparked desires, like stars in flight,
Chasing shadows, embracing night.
A sorcerer's touch upon the ground,
With every flicker, secrets found.

The mystique shrouded in the dark,
Awakens souls, ignites the spark.
Beneath the surface, hidden flames,
Unraveling the world's lost names.

From cinders rise, a haunting song,
In whispers soft, where we belong.
With magics brewed from ash and dust,
In smoldering sorcery, we trust.

Twilight's Carried Charcoal Charm

In twilight's hush, the forest glows,
A charcoal charm that softly flows.
Where shadows merge, and secrets hide,
Mysteries dance on the silken tide.

Flickering lights, like fireflies play,
Guiding spirits on their way.
With every pulse, the magic hums,
A symphony where silence drums.

Carried forth on the gentle breeze,
Echoes of time stir with ease.
In moments captured, past and new,
Charcoal charms in every hue.

Whispers linger in the midnight air,
Where dreams converge, and none compare.
In shadows cast, the heart will yearn,
For twilight's glow and the lessons learned.

Beneath the stars, the spirits weave,
A tapestry that we believe.
In every flicker, a tale to tell,
Of twilight's charm, cast under spell.

Alchemy Beneath the Burnt Vault

Beneath the vault, where spirits dwell,
In burnt remains, the secrets swell.
Alchemy brews, both rich and rare,
Transforming ashes into air.

The olden lore, a mystic guide,
In molten gold, our fears abide.
With every trial, the heart reborn,
From smoldered fate, the new is worn.

In scattered ruins lie the clues,
To rise anew from what we lose.
The fires of change, forever bright,
Ignite the shadows of the night.

Transcendence found in every spark,
Illuminating paths through the dark.
Beneath the vault, the stories start,
Of alchemy etched within the heart.

Through trials faced and lessons learned,
In ashes deep, the dreams are turned.
From burnt remains, a spark divine,
In alchemy's grasp, the worlds align.

Ink of the Smoldering Quill

In shadows cast by flickering flame,
The ink bleeds secrets, none to name.
Whispers linger, caught in the air,
Words of power, laid bold and bare.

A quill that dances, alive with fire,
Scribes the heart's most fervent desire.
Each stroke ignites, a timeless tale,
A parchment burned, but thoughts prevail.

Embers glow with forgotten lore,
The past awakes, it yearns for more.
Every line a bridge to the soul,
In this dark ink, we become whole.

The smoldering quill speaks with might,
Revealing shadows that haunt the night.
With every word, a world unfolds,
In the heart of the brave, truth beholds.

So let it write, let the stories flow,
In smoldering depths, where wonders grow.
For in the ink, the fire stands,
A dance of fate in trembling hands.

The Sorcerer's Bane and Blessing

A sorcerer weaves with threads of fate,
In shadows deep, where secrets wait.
His spells a mix of bane and light,
Guiding the lost through endless night.

Wisdom gained, yet heavy the cost,
In each enchantment, a dream is lost.
For power sought can twist the soul,
A heart once pure, now plays the role.

From whispered chants to casting signs,
He walks the edge where chaos aligns.
Yet in the dark, a spark remains,
The blessing born from enduring pains.

The dance of magic, a fragile art,
In every choice, he maps the heart.
With every spell, both dark and bright,
He learns to trust the flickering light.

In the end, a tapestry spun,
Bane and blessing, forever won.
The sorcerer's tale, both sharp and clear,
A lesson carved from timeless fear.

A Tapestry of Whispers and Smoke

In the stillness of a waning night,
Whispers weave, cloaked in twilight.
Silken threads of forgotten dreams,
Entwined in shadows, or so it seems.

Beneath the stars, stories unfold,
Ancient secrets in silence told.
The smoke curls softly, painting the air,
A tapestry rich with stories rare.

Each sigh a chapter, each breath a line,
Binding the lost souls through space and time.
With every flicker, a memory glows,
In the heart of night, the truth slowly shows.

Laughter dances, sorrow finds peace,
In the tapestry, all spirits cease.
Threads of the past, woven with care,
A map of our lives, fragile yet rare.

Let the whispers guide us through the haze,
To discover the light in the darkest days.
For within the smoke, we find our way,
Through a tapestry spun, come what may.

Charred Riddles of the Void

In the heart of darkness, riddles grow,
Charred remnants of what we don't know.
The void whispers softly, beckoning near,
In every echo, the unknown sneers.

Questions linger in the burning night,
The answers fade, caught in the light.
Yet within the ash, truth hides profound,
In the silence, lost thoughts abound.

A flicker of hope in the shadow's embrace,
Each riddle a mask, a haunting face.
In the void, we search for the spark,
To illuminate paths through the dark.

Charred memories whisper of battles fought,
The lessons learned, the wisdom sought.
Yet still we stand, facing the deep,
In riddles woven, our fates we keep.

So we delve into the depths of despair,
Seeking the light, we continue to dare.
For in the void, both danger and grace,
We find our truth, our rightful place.

Riddles in the Remnants of Ruin

Whispers echo through stone halls,
Ancient stories in the walls.
Broken arches tell their tales,
Of lost kingdoms, shrouded veils.

Crumbled paths lead to the skies,
Time's shadow in every sigh.
Silent guardians holding ground,
In the debris, secrets found.

Fragments glint in golden light,
Each piece a hint of the night.
Where laughter once filled the air,
Now only ghosts linger there.

Memories dance in the dust,
In fate's canvas, faded trust.
Riddles formed in broken seams,
Echo softly through the dreams.

Yet, in ruin, beauty lies,
A canvas painted with soft cries.
In every shadow, stories bloom,
Riddles whispered in the gloom.

The Phantoms of Hatched Coals

Flickering flames in the night,
Phantoms weave in ghostly light.
Memories crackle like the fire,
Dancing spirits of desire.

Hatched coals breathe warmth and fear,
Whispers echo, drawing near.
Embers glow with tales untold,
Of hearts that once burned bold.

Silhouettes in the smoky haze,
Lost in night's mysterious maze.
A glance, a touch, a fleeting breath,
In these shadows, linger death.

Phantom flickers rise and fall,
A beckoning with their call.
As the night unfurls its seam,
The coals ignite forgotten dreams.

In the warmth, the truth reveals,
Heartfelt wishes beneath the heats.
Fear and joy, a fragile line,
In coal's darkness, spirits shine.

Enigma Woven in Fiery Veils

Threads of flame whisper and dance,
In fiery veils, they take their chance.
Colors blend, a tapestry grand,
An enigma spun by unseen hands.

Silken warmth shrouds the night,
Dreams entwined, a pure delight.
Ember eyes that see it all,
In the night's spellbound thrall.

Secrets bubble, truth ignites,
Mysteries held in the sights.
Each flicker a story begins,
In this realm where silence spins.

Veils of fire wrap the heart,
In their warmth, souls impart.
An enigma rich and bright,
Woven fine in the night's light.

Within the coals, hope is stowed,
A journey where love once flowed.
Fiery threads, delicate and deep,
In their embrace, secrets keep.

Shadows Cast by Wandering Sparks

Sparks dance high and shimmer low,
Casting shadows in midnight's glow.
Each flicker a fleeting grace,
In the darkness, dreams embrace.

Whispers of the fire's song,
Echo where the souls belong.
Wandering sparks, lost and found,
In the night, a soft surround.

Longing lingers in the air,
Shadows twirl as if to care.
Each spark a wish, a silent plea,
In the dark, they yearn to be.

A dance of light, a transient fate,
In shadows' fold, we contemplate.
Life's fleeting moments unfold,
In the warmth of ashes cold.

Beneath the heavens' vast expanse,
Where hope and shadows share a dance.
Wandering sparks in the night sky,
Sing a lullaby, a soft sigh.

Gusts of Charred Secrets

Whispers carried on the breeze,
From shadows deep, they tease.
Burnt remnants of a forgotten tale,
In the night, their echoes wail.

Secrets lingering in the smoke,
Each ember sparks, a silent cloak.
The past erupts with every gust,
In charred remains, we place our trust.

Veils of ash dance in the light,
Faint memories within the night.
Lost voices cry from the ground,
In the silence, truths are found.

Amidst the flames, shadows play,
Old regrets find their own way.
In the heat, we breathe the pain,
Gusts of fate, our hearts constrain.

These swirling winds, they hold the key,
To hidden things too dark to see.
In charred remains, we can't forget,
Gusts of secrets that linger yet.

Silence of the Ashen Cradle

In whispers soft, the night is still,
A cradle wrapped in ash and chill.
Where fire once warmed a tender soul,
Now silence reigns, a heavy toll.

The embers fade, yet shadows loom,
Within the hearth lies sorrow's bloom.
Soft echoes of dreams once bright,
Now hold their breath in fading light.

Once lively flames, now ghostly sighs,
In the stillness, the heart complies.
A tale unfolds in muted grace,
In ashen slumber, we find our place.

The cradle rocks, a gentle sway,
While memories in silence stay.
In every flicker, a promise kept,
In the quiet, the world has wept.

Through the gloom, a soft refrain,
Of whispered hopes and quiet pain.
In stillness dressed in soft dark lace,
The ash embraces time and space.

Mystical Sparks of Gloom

In the twilight's tangled web,
Mystical sparks twist and ebb.
Beneath the surface, shadows glide,
In the gloom, where secrets bide.

Flickers dance like lost desires,
Amidst the whispers of hidden fires.
Each spark a story left untold,
In the silence where dreams unfold.

Veils of night conceal the truth,
Chasing echoes of fading youth.
Within the dark, a promise glows,
As hope entwines where sorrow flows.

In shadows, the heart learns to yearn,
For the warmth of hope to return.
These sparks of gloom, a guiding light,
In the depths of the endless night.

Mystical threads of fate align,
With every flicker, dreams entwine.
In the dim, our spirits play,
Sparks of gloom lead the way.

The Hero's Smoldering Echo

In the aftermath of battles fought,
A hero's heart by embers caught.
Smoldering echoes linger near,
In the silence, we feel their fear.

Ashes whisper tales of old,
Of bravery and hearts bold.
Through the haze, their silence calls,
In smoldering depths, the sorrow falls.

Flickering flames of glory past,
In shadows deep, memories cast.
The lore we hold, a guiding flame,
In the stillness, we call their name.

A hero's tale, forever burns,
Through ages lost, the spirit turns.
In smoldering remains, we seek the light,
Through echoes of courage, we find our fight.

Each ember glows with stories vast,
Of heroes born, their legacies cast.
In the quiet, their fire stays,
In smoldering whispers, we hear their praise.

The Midnight Pyre's Reckoning

In the stillness of night, flames arise,
Whispers of sorrow, beneath the skies.
They dance with secrets, a flickering plight,
Echoes of souls, lost in the light.

Ashen remnants, tales untold,
Churning the depths of the fire's cold.
Fingers of smoke reach for the stars,
Binding the broken with unseen scars.

Time holds its breath, as shadows loom,
Each ember glows in the shroud of doom.
Visions of hope in the ashes' glow,
A reckoning found in the flames below.

Bright spirits flicker, then fade away,
Their cries intertwine in the night's ballet.
What once was whole, now scattered ash,
In the silence, we reckon the past.

Yet from these cinders, anew shall bloom,
Reviving the light from the ashes' gloom.
The signal of life, though lost in sight,
The pyre must burn to summon the night.

Ashes to Shadows

From the depths of embers, whispers rise,
Shadows of memories beneath the skies.
Each grain of ash holds a story old,
In the quiet dusk, their truths unfold.

With every flicker, a tale ignites,
Carved in the stillness of moonlit nights.
Fates intertwined in a dance of despair,
Breath of the past lingers in the air.

Sparks flicker, drawing pictures unseen,
Reflecting the glimmers of what might have been.
In the heart of the fire, souls intertwine,
In shadows they wander, through secrets divine.

Cloaked in the twilight, the heartbeats thrum,
A rhythm of echoes, where dreams succumb.
Yet hope is born in the quiet refrain,
Ashes to shadows, they'll rise once again.

Time's gentle hand cradles the night,
Guided by stars, absorbing the light.
From darkness to dawn, we seek to know,
The cycle of life, through the ashes' glow.

The Arcane Hand in Charcoal

In twilight's canvas, the charcoal swirls,
Marking the tales of forgotten worlds.
An arcane hand weaves stories untold,
In the depths of darkness, the light unfolds.

Fragile sketches whisper, bittersweet,
Echoing visions that time can't delete.
Each stroke a memory, vivid and stark,
Illuminating truths hidden in the dark.

A phantom's dance, beneath charcoal skies,
Fate etches patterns where silence lies.
The ink of time, a river that flows,
The arcane hand knows what the heart bestows.

With every stroke, the past screams alive,
Tales of despair and the will to survive.
In the gallery of shadows, stories reside,
The arcane hand is a guide, not a guide.

Through charcoal realms, we find our way,
Tracing the echoes of yesterday.
In every line, a journey begins,
An arcane dance where the light never thins.

Whispers of magic in every breath,
Life intertwined with the memory of death.
In charcoal realms, we forever stand,
Bound by the stories of the arcane hand.

Secrets of the Burnt Cauldron

Within the shadows, the cauldron brews,
A potion of secrets, old and infused.
With flickering flames, the whispers ignite,
Revealing the past in the dead of night.

A blend of shadows, moonlight, and tears,
Stirring the echoes of lost yesteryears.
For each brew summons ghosts from their rest,
As the secrets unfold in the heart's chest.

From the depths of the mix, the visions arise,
Lacing through dreams under starlit skies.
The cauldron sighs with a mystical breath,
Crafting the future, where hope conquers death.

In the simmering depths, what cannot be known,
Lies tangled in fate, and fear has grown.
The lessons we learn from the fires that burned,
Will guide our steps where our spirits yearned.

Beneath the surface, a world resides,
With mysteries tangled in tides and hides.
The burnt cauldron whispers, secrets it keeps,
In every simmer, a promise, it leaps.

So gather the courage, embrace the unknown,
The magic awaits, in the heart, it's grown.
In the cauldron's echo, our fates intertwine,
With each sacred secret, the magic will shine.

The Ashen Secrets of Runic Weavings

In shadows dark, the runes align,
Whispers trapped in ancient stone.
Each mark a tale of starlit sign,
A language lost, a silence grown.

Beneath the ash, the secrets sleep,
Veins of magic, cold and bare.
In hidden tomes, their echoes creep,
Awaiting minds that dare to dare.

With fingers trembling, stories wake,
The weavers' knots, a tethered fate.
Through time's embrace, old visions quake,
A dance of power, wise and great.

In candlelight, the runes ignite,
Their glowing paths weave through the night.
Unlock the door, release the sight,
And find the truth in dark delight.

So gather close, and hear the call,
Of ashen whispers from the past.
For in these runes, we rise or fall,
As secrets weave, our fates are cast.

Glow of Forgotten Ceremonial Flames

Upon the altar, embers rise,
A flicker from the days of yore.
Within their glow, the spirit sighs,
Recalling rites of lore and core.

Chanted prayers in smoky threads,
Draped in dust of faded time.
Each flame a heart, where memory spreads,
Beneath the stars, an ancient rhyme.

Forgotten voices in silence whisper,
As shadows play upon the stone.
The fire's dance, a ghostly drifter,
Bringing forth what once was known.

In circles drawn, the watchers kneel,
With reverence for the winds of fate.
Candles flicker, and sparks conceal,
The stories waiting to create.

So light the flame, and dare the night,
Let ceremonial song be heard.
For in this glow, we forge the light,
To pierce the veil with every word.

Smoke Rings of Eldritch Inquiry

In twisted air, the smoke takes flight,
A question born from unseen realms.
Circling high with ethereal might,
Each ring a thought that overwhelms.

Phantom echoes in the mist grow,
As whispered doubts break through the haze.
Beneath the surface, truths may flow,
Enticing minds to ponder, gaze.

Through pathways strange, our visions sail,
Where shadows twist and legends fade.
The eldritch dance, a haunting tale,
Unraveled slowly, fate conveyed.

With every breath, the secrets buy,
A fleeting glimpse of what's to come.
In smoke rings rising to the sky,
We dive into the world undone.

So linger here, and watch them fade,
These whispers borne of other ties.
In every swirl, a truth portrayed,
To stir the mind and warm the eyes.

Sorcery in Remnants of Red and Gold

Amidst the leaves of autumn's thread,
Where crimson dances 'neath the trees.
The magic sways, both fierce and dread,
In whispered vows upon the breeze.

Golden glimmers spark the earth,
As twilight drapes its gentle shawl.
Each scattered leaf, a tale of birth,
Of secrets whispered through the fall.

With every step on ancient ground,
The air thickens with foreboding.
In remnants lost, the truth is found,
A choice to forge, or to be eroding.

Through lingering dusk, the sorcery gleams,
In bold strokes of a sunset close.
The final sigh of fleeting dreams,
A tapestry of life engrossed.

So weave your spell and cast it wide,
With reds and golds, your heart's delight.
In nature's lore, let magic bide,
As night encroaches, hungry for light.